Original title:
Echoes of the Inner Nebula

Copyright © 2025 Swan Charm
All rights reserved.

Author: Sabrina Sarvik
ISBN HARDBACK: 978-1-80561-324-4
ISBN PAPERBACK: 978-1-80561-885-0

The Reverberation of Radiant Light

In shadows cast by morning's gleam,
Whispers dance in golden streams.
Each ray a story softly told,
A tapestry of hues so bold.

Through every prism, laughter sings,
Awakening the joy it brings.
Colors swirl in joyous flight,
Echoes of the radiant light.

Drifting through Infinite Silence

In vastness where the stillness lies,
Stars shimmer in the endless skies.
With every breath, a calm embrace,
Time dissolves in this sacred space.

Fleeting thoughts like clouds above,
Whispers of the universe's love.
Drifting through the quiet night,
Lost in dreams, we take our flight.

Celestial Rhapsody in Darkness

In a veil of inky despair,
Notes of starlight fill the air.
Melodies from ages past,
Harmony that holds us fast.

With every pulse, the shadows sway,
Guiding dreams along the way.
In this dance of twilight's grace,
We find hope in the dark's embrace.

Remnants of Cosmic Legacies

In the dust of stars once bright,
Echoes linger in the night.
Memories of what has been,
Whispers in the cosmic din.

Fragments of time, a fleeting trace,
Carry stories through endless space.
In every heartbeat, whispers call,
The legacies of one and all.

Chronicles of the Ethereal Depths

In the vast weave of night,
Dreams dance in silver light.
Whispers ride the cosmic streams,
Echoing forgotten dreams.

Stars, they flicker like lost souls,
Guardians of ancient scrolls.
Tales of worlds both near and far,
Written in the light of stars.

Galaxies spin, a gentle sigh,
Beneath the velvet sky.
We dive into the unknown deep,
Where time and mystery sleep.

Nebulae bloom in colors bright,
Painting the canvas of night.
Each pulse of space, a heartbeat strong,
Strings of fate where we belong.

From shadows rise the dreams we chase,
In the ethereal embrace.
Together we write, together we soar,
In the depths, forevermore.

Tides of Celestial Memory

Waves of light, they ebb and flow,
Carving paths in cosmic glow.
Memories pulse like distant stars,
Shaping time, erasing scars.

Each moment drifts on azure tides,
Where the universe confides.
Whispers of ages long gone by,
Echo softly in the sky.

The moon reflects a tale untold,
In its embrace, the night grows bold.
Stars like dreams, they intertwine,
In the depths of the divine.

Celestial winds softly play,
Singing songs of yesterday.
Through the cosmos, we will roam,
Finding in shadows our true home.

With every wave, we ride our fate,
In love with time, we hesitate.
Eternal dance of memory's song,
In the tides, we truly belong.

The Poetry of Starborn Whispers

In the silence of twilight's grace,
Whispers come from a distant space.
Each star a word, each comet a phrase,
Crafting poems of luminous ways.

Through the cosmos, secrets flow,
In the heart of the ethereal glow.
Voices of light, tender and bright,
Writing tales in the fabric of night.

Eternity hums a soft tune,
Beneath the watchful eye of the moon.
Stardust weaves through our dreams,
Binding together heavenly themes.

Galactic voices call us near,
Carrying hopes, washing away fear.
In the poetry of the night sky,
Our spirits dance, as we fly high.

With every breath, we find our rhyme,
In the orchestrated flow of time.
Starborn whispers, a sacred art,
Echo through the chambers of the heart.

Pursuing Cosmic Shadows

Through cosmic realms, where shadows play,
We chase the light of a dawning day.
In galaxies, we weave our fate,
Following paths where starlight waits.

Veils of darkness cloak our quest,
Yet in the unknown, we find our rest.
Mysteries whisper in the night,
Guiding us toward the light.

In the void, where dreams collide,
A dance of shadows, side by side.
Each step forward, a heartbeat bold,
As the universe's secrets unfold.

Stars align in a celestial tune,
Crafting dreams beneath the moon.
We pursue the shadows, hand in hand,
In this cosmic dance, we make our stand.

With every breath, we dare to roam,
Through the vastness, we find our home.
Pursuing shadows, born of light,
Together we leap into the night.

Resonance in the Galactic Silence

Whispers of stars in the night,
Echoing dreams take their flight.
Silent worlds beyond our gaze,
In cosmic dance, time softly sways.

Fragments of light through the dark,
Guiding souls, igniting a spark.
Mysteries held in velvet deep,
Stories of ages, secrets to keep.

Celestial spheres in rotation,
Spinning tales of creation.
Harmony found in the void,
In resonant tones, peace is enjoyed.

Galaxies weave a tale so grand,
Hand in hand with the grains of sand.
Melodies lost, yet still they call,
In the silence, we rise or fall.

Each heartbeat ties us to the sky,
In its rhythms, we learn to fly.
Vibrations of love in the still,
Resonance flows, a divine will.

Illuminated Pathways to the Unknown

Beneath the glow of ancient lights,
Paths unfold, revealing sights.
With every step, shadows recede,
Curiosity sparks a new seed.

Whispers of wisdom softly gleam,
Guiding us through the twilight dream.
Footprints tread on uncharted trails,
In the silence, adventure prevails.

Colors burst in the darkening skies,
Sparks of hope where our spirit flies.
Unraveled mysteries beckon us near,
Embracing wonders, we conquer fear.

Voices echo in the void's embrace,
Calling forth dreams we dare to chase.
Hearts entwined in the stories spun,
Together we illuminate the run.

Each pathway leads to realms untold,
In the unknown, our fate unfolds.
Walking forward, with eyes aglow,
The luminous journey begins to flow.

Harmonics of a Celestial Mind

Within the cosmos, thoughts take flight,
Harmonies woven in the quiet night.
Each thought a star that brightly burns,
In the silence, wisdom returns.

Echoes of voices from worlds afar,
Guide the way like a distant star.
Melodic pulses in the air,
Consciousness dances without a care.

Synapses fire, light travels fast,
In the mind's cosmos, futures are cast.
Each moment infused with a sound,
In the depths, new echoes are found.

Minds as vast as the galaxy's sway,
In the dreamscape, we find our way.
Unified whispers of timeless lore,
Beyond the known, we long for more.

Harmonics resonating through time,
In the vastness, our spirits climb.
Transcending limits, embracing the kind,
In the silence, we seek and find.

Pulsing Hearts of Nowhere

In the stillness, hearts beat as one,
Pulsing softly, beneath the sun.
Nowhere lands, yet everywhere found,
In quiet places where dreams abound.

Rhythms echo in the emptiness,
Whispers of love in silent caress.
Footsteps wander without a trace,
Yet souls connect in eternal space.

Moments that linger, softly embrace,
Fleeting visions we cannot chase.
In the vastness, we find our home,
Through boundless realms, we freely roam.

A heartbeat shared, a breath of life,
Ties us all amidst the strife.
In nowhere's land, existence thrives,
Through pulsing hearts, true love survives.

Time stands still as we pulse and flow,
In connection, we learn and grow.
Nowhere blossoms, yet everywhere's sound,
In the heart's rhythm, all is profound.

Silhouettes of Distant Galaxies

In the night, they softly gleam,
Shadows dance in cosmic stream.
Whispers of a bygone light,
Stories told from endless flight.

Nebulas in hues so bright,
Paint the canvases of night.
Each a world, a tale untold,
In the fabric, stars unfold.

Echoes of a time long passed,
In these visions, shadows cast.
Journey far through astral seas,
Find the dreams in cosmic breeze.

Beyond the reach of mortal eyes,
Galaxies in silent skies.
With each twinkle, hope ignites,
Guiding hearts through starry flights.

Refractions of Time in Space

Moments bend, like light through glass,
A fragile dance, as seconds pass.
Time's illusion, swirling slow,
In the stillness, ripples flow.

Fragments echo, whispers clear,
Stories buried, dreams draw near.
In the void, we chase the light,
Reflections of our fleeting fright.

Galaxies spin, eternally,
In the weave of history.
A tapestry of fate's embrace,
Threads entwined in vastest space.

Each heartbeat marks a cosmic tone,
In the silence, we're not alone.
With every breath, we chart the way,
Through timeless nights, to brighter days.

Spheres of Thought Among the Stars

In silence deep, ideas bloom,
Each thought a star in velvet gloom.
Spheres of dreams collide and merge,
In the cosmos, our minds surge.

Cosmic whispers shape and mold,
Stories echo, bright and bold.
With every flicker, minds align,
In this vastness, thoughts entwine.

Through the void, our hopes take flight,
In constellations, find the light.
Bound together, we explore,
Spheres of wonder evermore.

Journeying through these realms unknown,
Among the stars, we find our own.
With every idea reaching far,
Touching realms like distant stars.

Harmony of the Astral Silence

In the void, a song is played,
Harmonies in soft parade.
Silent echoes, deep and wide,
In stillness, where dreams abide.

Nebulous notes, a soft caress,
Whisper secrets, gently press.
Calm envelops, shadows sway,
In the night, the heart finds way.

Beneath the stars, we pause and breathe,
In astral peace, we find reprieve.
United in this tranquil place,
Joyful silence, vast embrace.

As galaxies in rhythm spin,
We blend our souls, let journeys begin.
In harmony with night's sweet tune,
Together we dance beneath the moon.

Whispers in the Celestial Veil

In twilight's hush, shadows blend,
Secrets held, spirits send.
Stars awaken, softly glow,
Murmurs drift where night winds blow.

Veils of silver, softly spun,
Dance of dusk, day's undone.
Laughter echoes through the dark,
Guided by a fleeting spark.

Fleeting whispers, ancient songs,
Tales of where the heart belongs.
Each heartbeat a faded trace,
Lost in time, in endless space.

Galaxies swirl, secrets find,
In the vastness, love aligned.
Nebulae bloom in the night,
Cradled close, soft and light.

In the quiet, dreams take flight,
Beneath the watchful, starry light.
Whispers linger, shadows play,
In the celestial, night and day.

Murmurs of the Cosmic Abyss

Deep within the void's embrace,
Echoes linger, leave a trace.
Darkness hums a mellow tone,
In the silence, we're not alone.

Planets spin in ballet slow,
Murmurs rise from depths below.
Waves of time, they ebb and flow,
Secrets that the stars bestow.

From the depths, a voice does creep,
Through the shadows, secrets seep.
All the worlds yet to explore,
Waiting just beyond the door.

Eclipsed by mystery and light,
In the dark, there's pure delight.
Cosmic winds, they dance and twirl,
Through the abyss, life starts to unfurl.

Murmurs woven through the night,
Bring the silent dreams to sight.
In the darkness, we can hear,
Whispers floating, drawing near.

The Silent Dances of Stardust

In forgotten realms, stardust sways,
Silent dances through endless days.
Fragments of dreams in twilight's hue,
Falling softly, a cosmic dew.

Galaxies waltz in the night,
A radiant show, pure delight.
Each particle knows its place,
In the vast, eternal space.

Whirls of light, a gentle spin,
Echoes of what has always been.
Softly glimmering, tales unfold,
In the warmth of the starlit cold.

From dust we came, to dust we'll go,
In cosmic rhythms, secrets flow.
Each shimmer carries a silent plea,
Echoing through infinity.

In the silence, stardust beams,
Woven through our deepest dreams.
Dances whisper to the heart,
Binding us, though we're apart.

Reflections in Galactic Dreams

In the mirror of the night sky,
Galaxies twirl, and dreams fly high.
Reflections painted in cosmic streams,
Echoes of our most cherished dreams.

Cascading light from distant stars,
Whispers float, erasing scars.
In twilight's glow, we search for more,
Through the endless, open door.

Floating through the vast expanse,
Every moment, a fleeting chance.
Life and love, in starlight sewn,
In the galaxy, we are not alone.

Mirrored thoughts on cosmic waves,
Each heartbeat, the universe saves.
In the depth of night, we see,
All the truths that set us free.

Reflections glow, and dreams align,
In the darkness, you are mine.
In each glimmer, in each sigh,
We unite beneath the sky.

Invocations of the Celestial Mind

In the stillness of the night,
Thoughts like stars take flight.
Whispers from the vast above,
Guide me with their light.

Encounters with the unknown,
Mysteries gently shown.
Through the veil of lucid dreams,
Wisdom's seed is sown.

Echoes dance in silence,
Woven threads of brilliance.
Each reflection sparks a thought,
A tranquil resilience.

Threads of time entwined,
Within the mind, we find.
Galaxies in every glance,
A tapestry designed.

From shadows to the light,
Awakening the sight.
In every cosmic heartbeat,
The universe ignites.

Dreams from the Starlit Abyss

In visions deep and wide,
Dreams in cosmic tide.
Floating through the velvet night,
On starlight I ride.

Fragments of forgotten tales,
Whispered through the gales.
Infinity calls my name,
In echoing trails.

Silent secrets intertwine,
In realms where shadows shine.
The depth of space enfolds my soul,
In whispers so divine.

Beneath the celestial dome,
In darkness, I have roamed.
Each star a glimmer of hope,
Where dreams can find home.

With every wish I cast,
In the void so vast.
I reach for the impossible,
Where dreams forever last.

Conversations in the Cosmic Silence

In the silence of the stars,
Conversations from afar.
Each heartbeat swells with wonder,
In the night's memoir.

Through the quiet void we speak,
In whispers soft and meek.
The cosmos breathes around us,
In every word we seek.

Glances shared like shooting stars,
Unseen by earthly bars.
In unity, we traverse space,
Embracing who we are.

In timeless realms we linger,
With dreams that softly finger.
The tapestry of being,
In patterns that shimmer.

An infinite expanse to explore,
Where silence holds the core.
In conversations with the night,
We learn there's always more.

The Secret Life of Celestial Bodies

In the dark, they dance and spin,
Whispers of light from worlds within.
Silent stories in the night,
Secrets bound by the veil of light.

Winds of time and ancient lore,
Planets wander, forevermore.
Moonbeams cloak their hidden ways,
Eternal tales of cosmic plays.

Galaxies swirl in silent grace,
Touching softly, their vast embrace.
In the void, they breathe and sigh,
Sending messages through the sky.

Stars ignite in brilliant hues,
Painting the canvas with their views.
A ballet of spheres in the night,
Each holds wonders out of sight.

Floating in a velvet sea,
Timeless secrets, wild and free.
In harmony, they gently reside,
The secret life they cannot hide.

Rhythms Beneath the Starlit Dome

Underneath this vast expanse,
Celestial bodies take their chance.
With every pulse and every beat,
The universe sways, soft and sweet.

Echoes of light, they play along,
An ancient hymn, a cosmic song.
Melodies of darkness and light,
Resonating through the night.

Planets march in celestial lines,
Across the sky, the rhythm shines.
Synchronized, they weave and twine,
In a dance, both fierce and fine.

Comets streak with fiery tails,
Carving paths and making trails.
A symphony of the grand design,
Beneath the stars, their music aligns.

The moon hums low, the sun beams bright,
Together they craft the day and night.
In this dome, all life does thrive,
Syncopated, we come alive.

Illuminations from the Cosmic Beyond

Glimmers and glows extend their reach,
A radiant touch, the stars do teach.
From the void, their stories shine,
Guiding lost souls through their design.

Nebulas bursting with color and light,
Painting the cosmos, a magical sight.
Brilliance scattered, a celestial quilt,
In every thread, history built.

Auroras dance in vibrant bands,
Nature's light show, the heavens' hands.
Across the universe, they unfold,
Mysteries of the brave and bold.

Through the dark, a compass bright,
Leading the wanderers with delight.
Illuminations that never fade,
Stories in stardust, hand-crafted trade.

From black holes to supernova cries,
In every corner where wonder lies.
The cosmic beyond sings its song,
In its embrace, we all belong.

Conversations Among Celestial Bodies

In the silence, they exchange their tales,
Echoes of light that float like gales.
Moon to planet, star to sun,
Whispered secrets, two become one.

Comets share their journeys long,
While galaxies hum a celestial song.
With every orbit, stories weave,
In the fabric of time, we believe.

The sun laughs with a golden grin,
While shadows deepen, the night begins.
Each twinkle holds a word unspoken,
From the heavens, none are broken.

Planets nod in thoughtful grace,
Through the cosmos, they find their place.
Stars twirl, as laughter rings,
In the kingdom of celestial things.

They converse in rhythms only they know,
Guiding each other as they glow.
In the silence, friendships bloom,
Among celestial bodies, there's always room.

Orbiting Memories in the Milky Way

In the shadow of stars, whispers flow,
Fragmented dreams in celestial glow.
Each twinkle a tale, a moment in space,
Lost in the depths, where time leaves no trace.

Galaxies spin with a silent embrace,
Echoes of laughter, a shared warm place.
Floating on stardust, we wander so free,
Caught in the orbits of what used to be.

Through cosmic tunnels, we drift and we glide,
In the heart of the night, where memories bide.
The past and the present, a delicate weave,
In the Milky Way's arms, we learn to believe.

Lost in the vastness, we chase after dreams,
Fleeting reflections, like shimmering beams.
Navigating shadows, we search for the spark,
Orbiting memories, igniting the dark.

In the silent embrace of the universe wide,
Time flows like rivers, we learn to abide.
Each star holds a secret, each night tells a tale,
Orbiting memories, we dance in their trail.

Starlit Chambers of the Heart

In chambers of silence, where echoes reside,
Whispers of love in the shadows confide.
Stars in the distance, they shimmer and sigh,
Holding our secrets, in twilight they lie.

Every heartbeat a shimmer, every breath a flare,
Cosmic connections in soft, tender air.
In the starlit embrace of the night so divine,
We wander through dreams, your hand gently mine.

Deep in the cosmos, our journeys entwined,
Each pulse of the heart, to the universe blind.
In starlit chambers, our spirits take flight,
A dance through the darkness, abandoned to light.

Memories flicker, like comets so bright,
Awakening passions, igniting our night.
As constellations form paths we will chart,
Guided by starlight in chambers of heart.

Through ever-expanding, celestial tide,
In each starlit moment, our worlds coincide.
In the tapestry woven of love's tender art,
We find our forever in chambers of heart.

Vibrations of a Silent Cosmos

In the stillness of night, a soft pulse is felt,
Vibrations of cosmos, as darkness has dealt.
The whispers of galaxies echo and sway,
In the tranquil embrace of this timeless ballet.

Floating through silence, we dance with the stars,
Where gravity beckons and hope heals the scars.
The cosmos, a mirror reflecting our souls,
In vibrations of stardust, the universe trolls.

Like ripples in water, the moments collide,
Feel the heartbeat of space, where secrets reside.
Every twinkle a song, every shadow a clue,
Vibrations of silence in a cosmos so true.

Guided by wonders that shift in the dark,
Each note of existence ignites a small spark.
In vastness we linger, in stillness we play,
Embracing the vibrations of a silent array.

The universe whispers, as softly we tread,
In the spine of the cosmos, where echoes are fed.
Through infinite whispers, our spirits entwine,
Vibrations of magic in the fabric of time.

The Threads of Infinity Unraveled

In the labyrinth of stars, threads weave and unwind,
The fabric of time, a tapestry designed.
Whispers of ages, in shadows decay,
The threads of infinity call us to play.

Golden filaments shimmer in cosmic embrace,
Each strand a connection, each moment a grace.
Entangled in stories that stretch and expand,
The threads of existence flow through every hand.

As dawn breaks the silence, new patterns emerge,
Waves of creation in rhythmic surge.
The dance through dimensions, we weave and we sew,
In the threads of infinity, together we grow.

The universe pulses, a heartbeat in space,
Mapping our journeys, an eternal trace.
In the fabric of night, every spirit will twine,
The threads of infinity, forever aligned.

With every connection, new possibilities bloom,
In the garden of stars, dispelling the gloom.
Together we wander, hand in hand we travel,
Embracing the stories the threads have unraveled.

Phantoms in the Stellar Mist

In twilight realms where shadows play,
Whispers dance on cosmic winds,
Phantoms drift in the starlit sway,
Lost between what is and what rescinds.

Nebulae glow with secrets grand,
Flickers of dreams in night's embrace,
Guided by an unseen hand,
Fleeting forms in a timeless space.

Stars like jewels in velvet dark,
Illuminate the edge of night,
Each a tale, a distant spark,
Echoing thoughts that take to flight.

The lunar call, a soft lament,
Cascades through voids of endless grace,
Where silent hopes and dreams are sent,
O'er the canvas of cosmic space.

As nebulous tides begin to swell,
The dance of phantoms draws us near,
In stellar mists where wonders dwell,
We find the echoes of our fear.

Imagining the Hidden Cosmos

In the quiet swirl of twilight's breath,
Where dreams conjoin with starry streams,
Lies a universe of life and death,
Infinite realms that ignite our dreams.

Galaxies twine in a delicate weave,
Whispers of color in the night,
Imposing worlds that beckon and leave,
A canvas of wonder, pure delight.

With every pulse of the vibrant stars,
Stories unfold in ancient songs,
Creating bonds that heal our scars,
Unity within the cosmos belongs.

Through hidden paths where stardust flows,
Mysteries linger, softly sighing,
In the silence, a truth bestows,
An awakening, souls complying.

So let us soar on wings of light,
Imagining what lies beyond,
In the cosmos' enchanting flight,
We find our place and feel so fond.

The Language of Celestial Whirlpools

In the spiral dance of the cosmic seas,
Words unspoken begin to swirl,
Sung by the night in gentle breezes,
A symphony where the stars twirl.

Comets trace their paths with grace,
Scripted tales in the void of space,
Celestial whirlpools hold their place,
In rhythmic echoes, we embrace.

Through the lens of the interstellar night,
We share a language, pure and bright,
Speaking in hues, a sacred light,
Merging hearts and cosmic might.

Each star a word, each moon a phrase,
Crafting verses in eternal time,
In this celestial hymn, we gaze,
The universe whispers its rhyme.

Together we drift in this cosmic flow,
Understanding in the silence we know,
In the whirlpools where stardust glows,
We find the truth that binds us so.

A Reverie of Cosmic Murmurs

In the stillness of a galactic hush,
Reveries rise like soft-spun dreams,
Cosmic murmurs weave and rush,
Floating through whimsical beams.

Nebulous forms in the ether's dance,
Shimmering tales of longing glow,
In twilight's embrace, we lose our chance,
To grasp the wonders that overflow.

Bright auroras sing of the cosmos' birth,
Echoing notes of the past unseen,
A timeless ode to the very earth,
You and I in oneness, keen.

Each whisper dwells in tranquil night,
A tapestry woven with celestial thread,
With every spark, new worlds ignite,
And dreams entwined refuse to dread.

So let us linger in this gentle air,
Where cosmic murmurs softly call,
In reveries forged with tender care,
Together, we rise, together, we fall.

Etherial Lyrics of the Universe

In the vastness, stars collide,
Their light a song, a cosmic guide.
Whispers float on solar winds,
Dancing dreams where time begins.

Galaxies spin, a spiral grace,
Woven threads in endless space.
Nebulae bloom in colors rare,
They breathe a tale beyond compare.

Planets hum in silent glee,
A symphony of harmony.
Echoes of forgotten lore,
Sculpting paths we can't ignore.

Comets race with tails aglow,
Tracing patterns, ebb and flow.
In silence, secrets softly shared,
The universe, forever bared.

Amidst the void, a pulse we hear,
The beating heart of all we hold dear.
In every twinkle, every sigh,
A reminder of how we fly.

The Dance of Celestial Whispers

Moonlight drapes the night like silk,
Waves of quiet, deep and milky.
Stars in chorus, softly sway,
Guiding dreams that drift away.

In the stillness, shadows weave,
Tales of creation, hearts believe.
Galactic winds, a gentle tease,
Stirring whispers through the trees.

The cosmos spins, a velvet reel,
Unraveling truths that time can feel.
Eclipsed moments, fleeting sight,
Wrapped in the arms of starry night.

Constellations pierce the gloom,
A language birthed in endless bloom.
Their light a guide, a soft embrace,
In darkness, we find our place.

A dance of light, a swirl of fate,
In harmony, we resonate.
The universe whispers, wild and free,
In every heartbeat, a melody.

Patterns in the Astral Mist

Fog of stars drapes night's expanse,
Each glimmer holds a cosmic chance.
Patterns swirl, a timeless dance,
Drawing eyes into a trance.

Veils of light form a sacred space,
Where dreams and fears intertwine with grace.
Celestial bodies trace their flight,
Scripted in the fabric of night.

Colors blend in a silent swirl,
Ethereal tales of every girl.
Voices echo through the abyss,
A hymn of hope, a cosmic kiss.

The dance unfolds in stardust trails,
Unseen currents that softly sail.
Each breath a spark in galactic seas,
A reminder of how we believe.

Through the mist, we seek to find,
Threads that bind the heart and mind.
In the depths of the astral way,
Patterns whisper what they'll say.

Timeless Murmurs of the Dark

In shadows deep, where secrets lay,
Whispers drift, then fade away.
The moon, a sentinel of night,
Guides lost souls towards the light.

Stars together weave a tale,
Of dreams that soar, of hopes that sail.
An echo of the past, a spark,
Illuminates the boundless dark.

Celestial breath, a gentle sigh,
Stories linger as they fly.
In silence, wisdom finds its form,
A tranquil heart, a cosmic storm.

Each shadow hums a life once bright,
Fleeting glimpses in the night.
Timeless murmurs, deep and wide,
Remind us love can never hide.

The universe, a canvas vast,
Painted with memories of the past.
In every heartbeat, every spark,
We find our way within the dark.

Promises of a Distant Dawn

In the whisper of night, dreams take flight,
Soft echoes of hope, shining bright.
Each promise a spark, in dark's long embrace,
Awakening hearts, to time and space.

With every new day, the shadows fade,
Gentle rays emerge, a warm cascade.
Winds of change bring a tender kiss,
Filling the soul with newfound bliss.

Through valleys of doubt, we will tread,
Chasing the light, where dreams are bred.
A canvas awaits, colors to blend,
In the dawn's embrace, our spirits mend.

The horizon calls, with glimmers of gold,
Whispers of stories waiting to unfold.
Each breath a promise, a fresh start anew,
In the radiant dawn, we'll find what is true.

Luminous Reflections of the Soul

In quiet waters, reflections gleam,
A dance of the heart, a shimmering stream.
Each ripple a whisper, secrets untold,
Capturing moments, both brave and bold.

The moonlight weaves through the trees so tall,
Echoes of laughter, a gentle call.
In the depths of stillness, we find our way,
Time melts like wax, with each passing day.

Eyes locked in silence, an ethereal thread,
Binding our spirits where words dare not tread.
In each fleeting glance, a universe shines,
Stars twinkle softly, in celestial lines.

Every heartbeat resonates, a tune divine,
In harmony's embrace, our souls intertwine.
Together we rise, through shadows and light,
Luminous reflections, burning ever bright.

The Silence Between Stars

In the vastness of night, silence reigns,
A tapestry woven, in dark, it sustains.
Every twinkle a pause, a moment held tight,
Echoes of dreams in the stillness of night.

The cosmos whispers, secrets it knows,
In quietude, life's true beauty flows.
Galaxies spinning, in tranquil ballet,
Holding the stories that time won't betray.

Between every star, a heartbeat alive,
In the silence, we flourish, we thrive.
The void sings a song, mysterious and deep,
A lullaby gentle, inviting our sleep.

Where darkness lingers, hope finds a way,
In the silence of stars, we'll find where we stay.
An infinite journey, riding the beams,
In the stillness of space, we'll weave our dreams.

Constellations of Forgotten Thoughts

In the corners of minds, old memories hide,
Constellations of thoughts, scattered wide.
Each glimmer a tale, lost in the haze,
Threads of existence, in time's gentle gaze.

Whispered reflections, echo in the soul,
Mapping the journeys that make us whole.
With every starlit night, shadows reveal,
The fragments of dreams, remnants of zeal.

Unraveled stories dance in the dark,
Flickers of passion, igniting a spark.
As constellations merge, new paths align,
Forgotten thoughts bloom, blooming divine.

In the space of a breath, they come alive,
Carrying the wisdom from which we derive.
Through the whispers of time, we'll find our way,
In the constellations, forever we'll play.

Threads of Light in the Darkness

In shadows deep, where silence lies,
A glimmer breaks, a whisper sighs.
Threads of hope in woven night,
Weaving dreams, igniting light.

Stars above in cosmic glow,
Guide our hearts where we must go.
Each thread spun with love's embrace,
Illuminating time and space.

Through every tear, a spark will bloom,
A testament to chase the gloom.
In darkest hours, we must believe,
That from the dark, we can receive.

As dawn approaches, fears unwind,
In every shadow, strength we find.
Threads of light, our paths unite,
In the tapestry of the night.

Embrace the glow when hope feels thin,
For where there's light, there's love within.
Together we will rise and soar,
Threads of light forevermore.

Adrift in the Cosmic Stream

Floating softly on the breeze,
Ethereal winds carry dreams with ease.
Stars like pearls scatter the sea,
Adrift in the cosmic flow, we're free.

Galaxies whirl in a dance so grand,
We're mere specks in this vast land.
With each heartbeat, the universe calls,
In its embrace, our spirit enthralls.

A journey etched in time and space,
Through stardust trails, we find our place.
Nurtured by light, we gently sway,
In this cosmic stream, we drift away.

Currents of time, relentless and vast,
Whispering secrets of ages past.
In silence deep, we draw our breath,
Connected forever, defying death.

Together we flow, united as one,
Adrift in the stream, beneath the sun.
Cosmic travelers, we'll find the way,
Navigating the stars, come what may.

The Serenity of Forgotten Stars

In the quiet, the echoes fade,
Whispers of past where dreams once played.
Forgotten stars, in silence they gleam,
Guardians of hope, keeping agleam.

Ghosts of light in seductive hush,
They carry tales of the cosmic rush.
A lullaby woven in threads of night,
Cradled softly, holding pure light.

Their stories linger in the dark,
A tranquil dance, an eternal arc.
Though time may hush their glowing flames,
Their essence lives in endless claims.

In solitude, the heart takes flight,
Chasing the glow of that distant light.
In the vastness where answers sleep,
The serenity, a promise to keep.

Through the ages, our spirits soar,
Embracing the stillness, yearning for more.
Forgotten stars, we'll hold you dear,
In your serenity, we persevere.

Fables within the Cosmic Whisper

In whispers soft, the cosmos sings,
Stories of life and other things.
Fables woven in twinkling light,
Echoes of dreams that take flight.

Each star a tale, each moon a sigh,
Endless wonders that drift and fly.
Fables that dance on celestial streams,
Guiding our hearts with luminous beams.

The constellations tell of old,
Legends of brave, and stories bold.
In the hush, the galaxies weave,
Whispers of magic for those who believe.

Through time and space, the fables glide,
Carried by stardust, they spread wide.
With every heartbeat, whispers grow,
Stories of love in the starlit flow.

So listen closely, let your heart free,
Within the night, your dreams can be.
For every whisper in the dark,
Holds a fable, a glowing spark.

The Mind's Journey Through the Cosmos

In silent nights, the stars align,
A million thoughts in endless time.
Each whisper speaks of dreams untold,
A cosmic dance, a sight to behold.

Within the depths of darkened space,
The mind takes flight, an endless race.
Galaxies swirl, and visions gleam,
A universe woven from a dream.

Through nebulous clouds and stardust trails,
The heart finds strength where reason pales.
A journey vast, where echoes roam,
In solitude, we find our home.

With every pulse, the rhythms flow,
Each heartbeat syncs with starry glow.
The pulse of worlds, the truth we seek,
In silence found, in shadows meek.

And when at last, the voyage ends,
The cosmos whispers, a friend transcends.
For every thought, a celestial spark,
In the mind's journey, we leave our mark.

Tales from the Stellar Wilderness

In the wilds of stars, a story thrives,
Where ancient whispers of the cosmos drive.
Each stellar bloom, a tale portrayed,
Of distant worlds and dreams delayed.

Through shimmering void, adventure calls,
In lunar valleys, where silence falls.
Galactic winds weave vibrant songs,
Echoing myths where each heart belongs.

The constellations share their lore,
Of battles fought and cosmic war.
Lightyears crossed, the brave have flown,
In stellar storms, their courage known.

With comets bright that streak the night,
They carry hopes on wings of light.
In every glint, a fable beams,
In cosmic yarns, we weave our dreams.

And in the void, a silence reigns,
Yet every star, a memory remains.
In the stellar wild, our spirits sway,
A boundless dance on night's ballet.

Whirling Through the Astral Depths

Through swirling mists, we drift and glide,
The cosmos beckons, our hearts collide.
In whirls of light, we find our place,
Among the gems of endless space.

With every turn, new wonders spark,
In astral depths, there lies the mark.
A journey spun on gravity's thread,
As dreams take form, where angels tread.

Nebula's hues, a painter's dream,
With every shade, our spirits beam.
Time bends softly, moments tease,
In this embrace, our souls find ease.

Galactic rivers flow and turn,
With every pulse, a heart will yearn.
In cosmic storms, we dance and sway,
Through astral depths, we find our way.

Thus whirling through, we carve our art,
In the vastness, we never part.
The universe calls, and we respond,
In whirling dreams, our souls are fond.

Sagas of the Forgotten Cosmos

In shadows deep, the stories hide,
Of cosmic realms where dreams abide.
A tapestry of time untold,
In every star, a memory bold.

Where ancient echoes softly sigh,
In whispered tales of days gone by.
Each nebula, a chapter's grace,
In the forgotten, we find our place.

Through endless voids, lost myths reside,
In silent cries, the past confides.
With comets' trails, the truths arise,
In distant glows, our fate lies.

The sagas of old in stardust spun,
In every journey, we become one.
Out in the cosmos, we seek to know,
The stories lost, where shadows grow.

And as we wander, we learn to see,
The age-old dance, our history.
In every fragment, the past aligns,
In the forgotten, our spirit shines.

The Call of the Luminescent Void

In the depths where silence sings,
Stars flicker, offering wings.
Voices echo, soft yet bold,
Whispers of the tales untold.

A trail of light leads the way,
Through shadows where dreamers sway.
A beckoning glow from afar,
Guides the seekers, like a star.

Upon the edge of nothingness,
Time wraps in a gentle caress.
Veils of night, shimmers of fate,
In the void, we contemplate.

With every pulse, a heartbeat near,
The cosmos hums, crystal clear.
In the vacant stretch we roam,
Finding in the void a home.

Let the luminescent dance begin,
As we lose ourselves within.
The call so sweet, forever bold,
In the nothingness, we behold.

Secrets in the Starry Canvas

Beneath the vault of twinkling lights,
The secrets whisper, take their flights.
Each star a brushstroke, bold and bright,
Painting dreams in the velvet night.

Shadows of stories long since past,
In hushed murmurs, the die is cast.
Galaxies weave their ancient thread,
In the tapestry where hopes are fed.

Planets spin in a dance divine,
Reflecting truths in cosmic line.
Wonders waiting to be revealed,
On this canvas, fate is sealed.

Glimmers of fate twine with despair,
Interstellar wonders, a shared prayer.
In the silence, we find our place,
With stardust dreams, we embrace.

The night unfolds its magic keen,
As we ponder what lies unseen.
Secrets dwelled in the cosmic sea,
In every sparkle, you and me.

Hymns from the Dark Matter Realm

In the void where shadows blend,
Whispers of time start to transcend.
Dark matter hums a lullaby,
A symphony beneath the sky.

Veils of mystery, silent and deep,
In cosmic womb, secrets keep.
In the dark, emotions swirl,
Every heartbeat's cosmic pearl.

Ethereal echoes, soft and sweet,
Fill the abyss with a heartbeat.
In this realm, we weave and spin,
Creating worlds from within.

Songs that linger beyond the sight,
Guide us through the fading light.
Each note a spark in endless flight,
Carving pathways through the night.

The dark matter sings with grace,
In the void, there's a sacred space.
Hidden hymns that softly flow,
Reveal the wonders we can't know.

Thoughts of Celestial Wanderers

In wanderlust, our spirits roam,
Across the stars, we find our home.
With every path, a new embrace,
In celestial lands, we trace.

Fleeting moments, glimmers bright,
Thoughts adrift in cosmic flight.
The starlit sky, our guiding map,
In boundless space, we take a nap.

Through the realms of dust and flame,
In wonder, we call out each name.
Eons pass with each heartbeat's call,
In infinity, we rise and fall.

As wanderers of the night,
We seek the truth within the light.
Bound by the dreams we share and sigh,
In the vastness, we learn to fly.

Thoughts collide in cosmic streams,
Echoes of our unspoken dreams.
As we traverse this endless space,
We find each other in the grace.

Celestial Echoing of Lost Dreams

In the quiet night sky, stars gleam,
Whispers of hopes drift, weaving a dream.
Echoes of laughter, shadows of tears,
Lost in the cosmos, beyond our years.

Winds of the past carry tales untold,
Fragments of wishes in stardust unfold.
Each twinkle a promise, a memory rare,
A cosmic reminder that love lingers there.

Galaxies beckon, with arms spread wide,
Questions of fate in the dark collide.
Where do we wander? Where shall we stay?
The universe listens, come what may.

Dreams dance like comets across the black,
Fleeting and bright, they follow no track.
Yet in their wake, they leave a trace,
A cosmic mirror of lost embrace.

So, in the silence, let echoes resound,
In the realm of stars, our dreams are found.
Celestial horizons, where wishes take flight,
In the heart of the cosmos, they shimmer in light.

Horizons of a Wandering Spirit

Beneath the sky, a spirit roams free,
Chasing horizons, where dreams yearn to be.
Each step a whisper, each turn a chance,
In the dance of the world, a fleeting glance.

Mountains rise high, valleys deep below,
Paths yet untrodden, only the brave know.
With the wind as a guide, and stars for a map,
In the heart of the journey, there's always a gap.

Oceans and rivers, they call out my name,
In landscapes of wonder, I seek the same.
The horizon stretches, a promise of light,
A canvas of colors in the embrace of night.

Time flows like water, ever so dear,
Moments are treasures, both far and near.
With every heartbeat, I feel the release,
The spirit of wandering, a dance of peace.

In the embrace of each sunrise anew,
Horizons unfold, painted in hues.
With the world as my stage, I step into fate,
A wanderer's heart, forever awake.

The Heartbeat of Starlit Existence

In the depths of night, silence prevails,
A heartbeat echoes, as starlight sails.
Each pulse a story, each throb a song,
In the tapestry of time, where we belong.

Dancing shadows beneath the glowing sky,
Fleeting moments that whisper and sigh.
The moonlight shimmer, a soft embrace,
Finding our rhythm in this sacred space.

Galaxies whirl in an endless embrace,
Each heartbeat a traveler through time and space.
We are but stardust in a fleeting glow,
Alive in the cosmos, forever to flow.

The spirit of night wraps us in dreams,
A symphony of silence, as starlight beams.
In the grand design of all that we see,
The heart of existence beats wild and free.

So let us listen to this cosmic tune,
In the heartbeat of starlight, beneath the moon.
We are the echoes, the whispers of night,
In the dance of existence, forever in flight.

Timelines Between Celestial Bodies

In the dance of planets, a tale unfolds,
Timelines intertwine, as each heart holds.
Moments converge in the void so vast,
Whispers of futures, shadows of past.

Stars align with a grace divine,
Tracing the paths where destinies twine.
Galactic tales in a cosmic sea,
Between celestial bodies, you and me.

Time bends softly, a delicate thread,
Woven in silence where dreams are led.
The rhythm of ages in orbit we find,
Links of existence, entwined and blind.

Constellations guide us through the night,
Charting the journeys in ethereal light.
With each pulse of time, we cross the divide,
In the embrace of the cosmos, we shall reside.

So let the stars map our way through dreams,
In the timelines where love always gleams.
Together we'll wander, through dark and bright,
In the cosmos together, a radiant flight.

The Symphony of Celestial Thoughts

In the night, stars whisper low,
Thoughts entwined, in cosmic flow.
Galaxies twirl, in perfect pace,
Every heartbeat finds its place.

Silent echoes, time's embrace,
Waves of wonder, through vast space.
Soaring dreams on starlit beams,
Life unfolding, like moonlit dreams.

Notes of light in dark's domain,
Melodies of joy and pain.
Each lost wish, a comet's flight,
Guiding souls through endless night.

Chorus of shadows, bright and bold,
Stories spinning, yet untold.
In the silence, wisdom speaks,
In every heart, the universe seeks.

Breaths within the Astral Canvas

Brush of stars on a velvet night,
Colors dance in gentle flight.
Every breath, a swirling hue,
Art of cosmos, pure and true.

Planets spin in vibrant grace,
Time and space, a wild embrace.
Each heartbeat strokes a story's line,
Original art, by design.

Nebulae bloom with hidden light,
Painting dreams within the night.
Every sigh, a brush of fate,
Every thought, a stroke innate.

Canvas stretches, vast and wide,
In its depths, our hopes reside.
From the ether, we are drawn,
To the beauty, dusk to dawn.

Journeys Through Celestial Shadows

In twilight's glow, we wander free,
Through shadows cast by memory.
Starlight guides our fleeting quest,
In the dark, we find our rest.

Whispers of the moonlit night,
Tell of dreams that take to flight.
Veils of night, so deeply spun,
Every shadow holds a sun.

Pathways wrought with tales of old,
Each step forward, brave and bold.
Through the dark, we chase the dawn,
In shadows deep, our fears are drawn.

Celestial maps, we navigate,
In the dark, we learn to wait.
Journeys lean on fate's hand,
In the silence, we understand.

The Unwritten Verse of the Universe

Lines unspoken, await the pen,
In the silence, we begin again.
Each star a word, each comet a phrase,
Within the void, the mind ablaze.

Epics lost in cosmic sea,
Waiting for our hearts to be.
Verses form in endless night,
Illuminated by inner light.

Unseen realms, a book untold,
Stories rich, yet uncontrolled.
In the quiet, dreams ignite,
Words of love, and tales of flight.

With each breath, the verse will flow,
Through the stars, we learn to grow.
Unwritten paths, we dare to trace,
In the universe, we find our place.

Whispers in the Cosmic Abyss

In darkness deep, the silence sings,
Among the stars, the lost heart clings.
Echoes swirl in the vast expanse,
Whispers of fate in a cosmic dance.

Galaxies twinkle, secrets await,
Among the shadows, we contemplate.
In the abyss, time bends and sways,
Guiding the dreamers through endless grey.

Fragments of light ignite the night,
Casting hopes on a distant flight.
In every shimmer, a story unfolds,
Of love and loss, of brave and bold.

The void hums with untold lore,
A lullaby from the ancient core.
Trailing whispers of cosmic might,
Into the depths, we seek the light.

So let us drift, lost in thought,
In the abyss, find what life sought.
With every whisper, a heart set free,
In the universe's vast tapestry.

Fragments of Stardust Dreams

In the cradle of night, stardust gleams,
Carrying echoes of hopeful dreams.
Fleeting moments slip through our hands,
In the cosmic sea, destiny stands.

Each twinkle tells a tale of yore,
A reflection of what we yearn for.
Souls entwined in a dance so divine,
In the starlight's embrace, our hearts align.

From shadows deep, aspirations rise,
Kissing the edges of endless skies.
Moonlit paths weave through the dark,
Guiding our spirits with dreams to embark.

Time is but a fleeting sigh,
In this vast expanse, we learn to fly.
Stars ignite the night's canvas bright,
Painting hopes in a spectrum of light.

As stardust settles on waking dawn,
We carry dreams as we journey on.
In fragments, we find what forever beams,
In the dance of time, in stardust dreams.

Celestial Reverberations

In the heart of night, echoes arise,
Songs of the cosmos, whispers in skies.
Celestial bodies in rhythmic embrace,
Painting the heavens with stirring grace.

Galactic symphonies play their tune,
Beneath the watchful gaze of the moon.
Every heartbeat finds its place,
In universal love, we trace.

Comets streak through, a momentary blaze,
Dancing through shadows, in stellar praise.
In reverberations, our spirits meld,
Bound by the stories the cosmos held.

In tranquil moments, silence speaks,
Language of stars in mystical peaks.
With every pulse, new worlds ignite,
In the dark's embrace, we unite.

So let us listen, let our souls soar,
To celestial whispers, forever more.
In the grand cosmos, a place for all,
In reverberations, we answer the call.

Chasing Shadows in the Void

In the still of night, shadows take flight,
Chasing the dreams that fade from sight.
Whispers ripple through the silent air,
In the void's embrace, we lose our care.

Echoes linger where light once danced,
In the folds of darkness, lost souls pranced.
With every step, the unknown calls,
Through empty realms, the spirit sprawls.

Horizon stretches, a blend of night,
Holding mysteries just out of sight.
As we wander through starless fears,
Courage ignites the path through tears.

With shadows as guides, we journey forth,
In the vastness, we seek our worth.
To find the light hidden within,
In the dark abyss, our story begins.

So let us chase what the void conceals,
In the quiet depths where the heart feels.
In shadows we find strength to reclaim,
Our place in the cosmos, our unyielding flame.

Resonance of the Astral Winds

In twilight's grasp, the stars align,
Whispers of night, soft and divine.
A fluttering breeze, the cosmos sighs,
Carrying secrets from distant skies.

Echoes of dreams ride the celestial flow,
Guiding lost souls where they long to go.
Each note a path, a twinkling thread,
Binding our hearts to the stories tread.

When shadows dance upon the shore,
A universe speaks, forevermore.
In the subtle hum, we find our grace,
In the astral winds, we find our place.

With every gust, memories swarm,
Wrap us in peace, keep us warm.
As night unfolds its velvet hue,
We listen close, and start anew.

So let us drift on this cosmic sea,
Knowing in stillness, we are free.
For in the winds, our souls ascend,
Connected through time, we transcend.

Soliloquies of Nebulous Nights

In soft murmurs, the cosmos speaks,
With nebulous clouds, and moonlit peaks.
A whispered thought, a tender song,
Where stardust dreams and echoes belong.

The night unfurls its velvet shroud,
As shadows weave, we sing aloud.
In the depth of darkness, light ignites,
A harmony born from countless fights.

The orbs of light trace paths of grace,
In solitude's arms, we find our space.
They tell of journeys and tales untold,
In every shimmer, a vision bold.

Beneath this dome of swirling art,
We etch our hopes, with beating heart.
Each breath a pledge to skies so wide,
In peaceful stillness, we confide.

So let us wander where wonders weave,
In soliloquies, we truly believe.
For each night's tale, a legend spun,
In the fabric of time, we are one.

Melodies Beneath the Cosmic Canopy

Beneath the stars, our spirits rise,
In whispers soft, they harmonize.
A gentle tune, a lullaby,
Carried on winds that drift and fly.

With every note, the universe sways,
Painting the night in a wondrous daze.
Celestial chords, vibrant and true,
Awaken the dreams that dwell in you.

As comets streak across the night,
A tapestry woven with pure delight.
The moonlight dances on silver streams,
While we lose ourselves in cosmic dreams.

In the soft glow of the cosmic dome,
We carve our names, we find our home.
Each sigh and laugh, a pulse of light,
In melodies shared, our souls unite.

So let us sway beneath the skies,
With every heartbeat, let us rise.
For in this music, we shall find,
A symphony woven through space and time.

Traces of Forgotten Constellations

In twilight's grasp, old tales appear,
Of constellations lost, yet near.
Their shapes enshrined in starlit lore,
Whispering secrets of days before.

Across the night, a canvas wide,
With stories hid, where dreams abide.
Each glimmer marks a path once bright,
In the depths of space, they still ignite.

The ghosts of stars weave through the past,
In shadows long and dreams amassed.
A dance of light, a fleeting trace,
Connecting hearts through endless space.

For in the cosmos, nothing fades,
But echoes linger in serenades.
As stardust whispers soft goodbyes,
We hold their essence in our eyes.

So let us search the skies above,
Finding in darkness, threads of love.
For in the traces, we rediscover,
The bonds of starlight, forever cover.

Phantasmagoria of Starry Thoughts

In the silence where dreams take flight,
Whispers of galaxies weave through the night.
Celestial echoes in a luminescent dance,
Painting the cosmos in a fleeting glance.

Wonders unfold in a shimmering stream,
Awakening visions lost to a dream.
Each spark of a star, a story to tell,
In the vast tapestry where mysteries dwell.

Nebulas cradle the hopes we release,
Galactic embraces bring comfort and peace.
Through the fabric of time, our wishes align,
Connecting our hearts in a celestial sign.

The moon's gentle gaze, a guardian bright,
Illuminates paths in the stillness of night.
With every heartbeat, the universe sighs,
A symphony woven through dark velvet skies.

Sketches of the Infinite Expanse

On the edges of dreams, where stardust paints,
Fragments of worlds dance like whimsical saints.
Galaxies twirl in a cosmic ballet,
Sketches of wonder in colors that play.

Whirling in silence, the nebulae bloom,
Channeling whispers that echo through gloom.
With each twinkle and flash, we journey afar,
Tracing our paths through the dust of a star.

From clusters of light, we weave our own fate,
Entangled in mysteries both grand and innate.
An infinite canvas where planets collide,
Sketching the dreams that the cosmos may hide.

In the depths of night, our spirits ignite,
Boundless and free, like a comet in flight.
Together we linger in the vast, endless glow,
Sketches of hope in an infinite flow.

Fragments of Cosmic Reverie

In the hush of the void, thoughts drift and sway,
Cascading through time in a dreamlike display.
Meteors fall as wishes collide,
Fragments of futures in mysteries hide.

Each twinkle a whisper of what could have been,
A glimpse of the infinite, hidden within.
We dance on the edges of time's gentle flow,
Gathering stardust wherever we go.

Eclipses embrace, shadows stretching wide,
Stitching the cosmos with secrets inside.
Through the void we wander, hearts open and free,
Fragments of reverie, just you and me.

With each passing star, stories unfold,
A tapestry woven from dreams yet untold.
In the embrace of the night's sweet decree,
We find the fragments of our cosmic spree.

Enigmas of the Starry Sky

Beneath the great dome where wonders reside,
Enigmas sparkle, a celestial guide.
Galactic riddles that tease and confound,
In the arms of the cosmos, mysteries abound.

With every glance, stories silently speak,
The riddles of time in shadows they seek.
Constellations twinkle, secrets in line,
Charting the path where the stars intertwine.

In the quiet, the universe hums,
Echoing soft as a heartbeat becomes.
Phantoms of space in delicate play,
Painting the night in an ethereal way.

Through spectra of colors that ripple and weave,
We chase every dream and dare to believe.
In the symphony sung by the starry tide,
Enigmas awaken, our spirits as guide.

Shadows of the Unseen Universe

In the void where echoes play,
Flickering stars hide away.
Whispers of dark matter sway,
Tales of night and endless day.

Galaxies bound in silent chains,
Cosmic dust in gentle rains.
Unraveled threads, forgotten names,
In shadowed spheres, no one reigns.

Beyond time's grasp, we wander wide,
Through realms where mysteries collide.
Lost in dreams we cannot snide,
In the dark, our hearts confide.

Light years pass, yet here we stand,
Holding on, hand in hand.
Across the stars, a vast command,
In the unseen, we understand.

Fleeting glimpses, visions rare,
In the night, we sense the air.
Shadows dance, a lover's snare,
In the depths, we linger there.

Voices from the Celestial Depths

Listen close, the stars are speaking,
Softly call us, gently seeking.
From the void, the echoes flow,
In the dark, their secrets glow.

Whispers deep, like flowing streams,
Carrying our forgotten dreams.
A cosmic choir fills the night,
Guiding souls with their pure light.

From the heavens, tales unfold,
Stories lost, yet never cold.
Voices weave through time and space,
In their chant, we find our place.

Mysteries wrapped in stardust veil,
Through the silence, hints prevail.
Each note sung, a sacred thread,
In their songs, our fears are shed.

Celestial calls, a timeless ring,
In the dark, our hearts take wing.
Find the path through night's embrace,
In the depths, we find our grace.

The Lullaby of Lost Starships

Drifting through the cosmic seas,
A lullaby carried on the breeze.
Starships lost, in shadows cast,
Echoes of a haunting past.

Whispers of the engines hum,
In the silence, memories come.
Tempered steel and dreams now fade,
In the darkness, plans are laid.

Drifting far from home's embrace,
Each starship holds a secret place.
Through the void, they wander slow,
Tracing paths we cannot know.

Galaxies weave a gentle song,
For the lost, to whom we belong.
In the night, they find their way,
Through the stillness, night and day.

Lullabies for those who roam,
In the stars, they find their home.
A timeless tune in endless flight,
Guides the ships into the night.

Chasing the Fragments of Light

Chasing light on endless plains,
Finding hope where darkness reigns.
Flickers spark in twilight's hold,
Stories untold begin to unfold.

Down the paths we yearn to trace,
Fragments gleam in cosmic grace.
Through the whispers of the void,
In each flash, our dreams deployed.

Shooting stars, a fleeting glance,
Invite us to the ancient dance.
Through shadows cast by fading day,
In the light, we find our way.

Burning bright, the stars align,
In their glow, the worlds combine.
Bringing forth the dawn of hope,
Inched closer, together we cope.

Fragments spark in nightly skies,
In their warmth, a new sunrise.
Together chasing, hand in hand,
Through the light, we understand.

Currents of Stardust Dreams

In the quiet night we drift,
Beneath a sky of ancient glow.
Whispers of worlds, soft and swift,
Carried where the soft winds flow.

Celestial streams of silver light,
Guide our hearts through endless sleep.
In the depths of starlit night,
Immerse in dreams both wide and deep.

Each twinkle holds a tale untold,
Of love and loss, of joy and pain.
In cosmic arms, we dare be bold,
For stardust binds us once again.

Together we weave our fate,
Dancing on the edges of time.
In the vastness, we resonate,
With the universe's subtle rhyme.

Shimmering hopes in silver beams,
Guide us through the dark unknown.
In currents of stardust dreams,
We find the paths we call our own.

Tales of the Starry Expanse

Across the tapestry of night,
Stories swirl in cosmic flow.
Galaxies swirl, a wondrous sight,
In tales of ages long ago.

Among the stars, the ancients speak,
Of journeys through the void so wide.
In every glance, our futures peek,
And in the heavens, we confide.

Constellations blink with ease,
Map our fate with quiet grace.
In the whispering evening breeze,
We seek the magic in this place.

Each moment wraps like silken threads,
Binding hearts to the cosmic glow.
In woven light, our spirit treads,
Where time and starlight intertwine and flow.

Together we'll chart the skies,
In this starry expanse, we'll roam.
Each tale a spark that never dies,
In the void, we've found our home.

Visions Woven in Starlit Nebulas

In nebulas where dreams take flight,
Colors dance in vibrant hues.
Visions spark beneath the night,
Painting paths for souls to choose.

Through veils of mist and radiant glow,
The cosmos whispers secrets shared.
In starlit realms our spirits flow,
As endless wonders are declared.

We are the echoes of the stars,
Woven in the cosmic seam.
Across the darkness, we chase far,
The fleeting shadows of a dream.

With every pulse, the universe sings,
A melody of hopes set free.
In the fabric of our beings,
Lies the beauty of eternity.

Together we wander, hand in hand,
Through the visions of the night.
In starlit nebulas, we stand,
Stories spun in radiant light.

Echoing Beneath the Cosmic Boughs

Underneath the cosmic boughs,
The universe sways with grace.
In shimmering light, we take our vows,
Finding comfort in this space.

With every star, a prayer we send,
In whispers carried on the breeze.
The heavens' beauty, our hearts commend,
In twilight's grace, we find our peace.

Met by shadows, we explore,
The vastness where our thoughts align.
Echoing dreams open every door,
To realms where time and starlight shine.

Through cosmic paths, we freely roam,
As constellations guide our way.
In silent night, we find our home,
Among the stars that softly play.

Underneath the arch of skies,
The echoes of our spirits weave.
In cosmic realms, where magic lies,
We share the dreams that we believe.

www.ingramcontent.com/pod-product-compliance
Ingram Content Group UK Ltd.
Pitfield, Milton Keynes, MK11 3LW, UK
UKHW021436220125
4239UKWH00039B/691